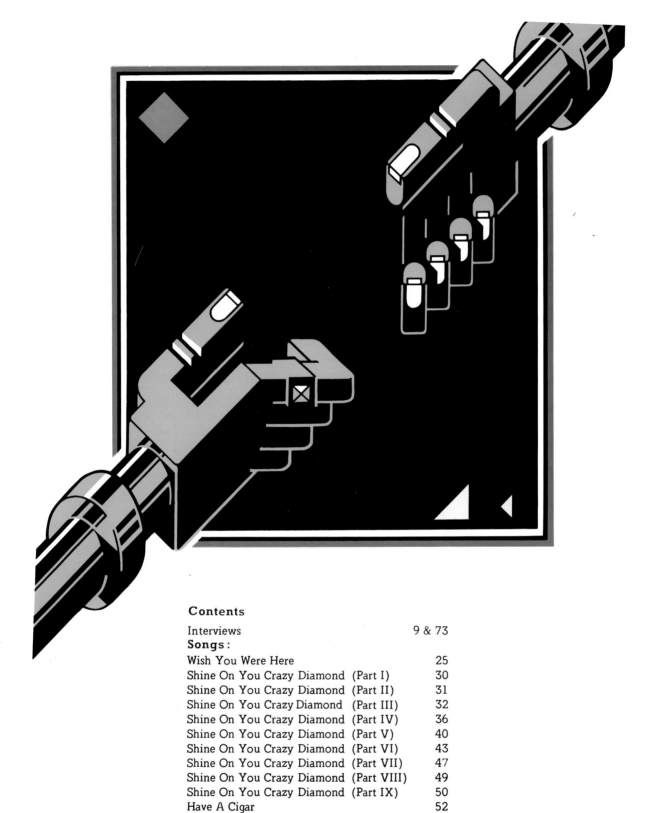

Contents

A Rambling Conversation with Roger Waters
concerning All this and that
Interviewed by Nick Sedgewick

N.S. Here's a good one to start with, Roger! Why was it two years before the Floyd made an album after Dark Side of the Moon?
R.W. . . . that's a very good question, I'm very glad you asked me that one . . . er . . .
Take your time . . . don't worry . . .
Without looking at diaries its very difficult. I'm trying to remember whatever went on . . . I'm not being funny, I honestly can't remember why. It was 1973 when Dark Side of the Moon came out wasn't it? January 1973, and we're now in Oct. '75, so in January '75 we began recording 'Wish you were Here' . . .
I remember I went to E.M.I. studios in the winter of '74, and the band were recording stuff with bottles and rubber bands . . . the period I'm talking about is the period before your French tour in June '74.
Ah! Right, yeah. Answer starts here . . . (great intake of breath) . . . Well, Nick . . . there was an abortive attempt to make an album not using any musical instruments. It seemed like a good idea at the time, but it didn't really come together. Probably because we needed to stop for a bit.
Why?
Oh, just tired and bored . . .
Go on . . . to get off the road? . . . have some breathing space?
Yeah. But I don't think it was as conscious as that really. I think it was that when Dark Side of the Moon was so successful, it was the end. It was the end of the road. We'd reached the point we'd all been aiming for ever since we were teenagers and there was really nothing more to do in terms of rock 'n roll.
A matter of money?
Yes. Money and adulation . . . well, those kinds of sales are every Rock 'n roll band's dream. Some bands pretend they're not, of course. Recently I was reading an article, or an interview, by one of the guys who's in Genesis, now that Peter Gabriel's left, and he mentioned P.F. in it. There was a whole bunch of stuff about how if you're listening to a Genesis album you really have to sit down and LISTEN, its not just wallpaper, not just high class musak like P.F. or 'Tubular Bells', and I thought, Yeah, I remember all that years ago when nobody was buying what we were doing. We were all heavily into the notion that it was good music, good with a capital G, and of course people weren't buying it because people don't buy good music. I may be quite wrong but my theory is that if Genesis ever start selling large quantities of albums now that Peter Gabriel their Syd Barrett if you like, has left, the young man who gave the interview will realise he's reached some kind of end in terms of whatever he was striving for and all that stuff about good music is a load of fucking bollocks. That's my feeling anyway. And 'Wish you were Here' came about by us going on in spite of the fact we'd finished.

What finally prompted a move back into the studio?

A feeling of boredom, I think really. You've got to do something. When you've been used to working very hard for years and years, and reached the point you were working towards there's still a need to go on because you realise that where you've got to isn't what you thought it was . . .

Was there some period during your apparent lay off when you all thought the band would come together almost 'of itself', and produce something?

It's so long ago . . . it's hard to remember, but I think there was that feeling . . . that somebody would eventually come up with something, an idea. The interesting thing is that when we finally did do an album the album (Wish you were Here) is actually about not coming up with anything, because the album is about none of us really being *there*, or being *there* only marginally. About our non-presence in the situation we had clung to through habit, and are still clinging to through habit — being P.F. Though its moving into a slightly different area again because I definitely think that at the beginning of 'Wish you were Here' recording sessions most of us didn't wish we were there at all, we wished we were somewhere else. I wasn't happy being there because I got the feeling we weren't *together*, the band wasn't at all together.

Stage by stage, how did the album happen?

We did some rehearsals in a rehearsal studio in Kings Cross, and started playing together and writing in the way we'd written a lot of things before. In the same way that 'Echoes' was written. 'Shine On You Crazy Diamond' was written in exactly the same way, with odd little musical ideas coming out of various people. The first one, the main phrase, came from Dave, the first loud guitar phrase you can hear on the album was the starting point and we worked from there until we had the various parts of 'Shine On' finished.

At the time the band was writing it, was the song for a tour or an album.

I'm glad you asked that, 'cos you've reminded me that in fact we were about to do a British Tour (Oct — Dec '74) and had to have some new material. So we were getting some things together for that.

There were a couple of other songs . . .

Yeah. 'Raving and Drooling' and 'You've Gotta Be Crazy'. 'Raving and Drooling' was something I'd written at home. Dave came up with a nice chord sequence, I wrote some words, and we carried on from there with 'You Gotta Be Crazy'.

It was then decided that these three songs would also be the basis for the forthcoming album?

Yes, that was the idea for a long time . . . while we did that tour.

When did the plans change?

When we got into the studio. January '75. We started recording and it got very laborious and tortured, and everybody seemed to be very bored by the whole thing. We pressed on regardless of the general ennui for a few weeks and then things came to a bit of a head. I felt that the only way I could retain interest in the project was to try to make the album relate to what was going on there and then *ie* the fact that no one was really looking each other in the eye, and that it

was all very mechanical . . . most of what was going on. So I suggested we change it — that we didn't do the other two songs but tried somehow to make a bridge between the first and second halves of 'Shine On', and bridge them with stuff that had some kind of relevance to the state we were all in at the time. Which is how 'Welcome to the Machine', 'Wish you were Here', and 'Have a Cigar' came in.

'Shine On' was originally a song concerning Barrett's plight, wasn't it?
Yes.

Do the other songs also fit in with that?
It was very strange. The lyrics were written — and the lyrics are the bit of the song about Syd, the rest of it could be about anything — I don't know why I started writing those lyrics about Syd . . . I think because that phrase of Dave's was an extremely mournful kind of sound and it just . . . I havn't a clue . . . but it was a long time before the 'Wish you were Here' recording sessions when Syd's state could be seen as being symbolic of the general state of the group, *ie* very fragmented. 'Welcome to the Machine' is about 'them and us', and anyone who gets involved in the media process.

And 'Have a Cigar'?
By taking 'Shine On' as a starting point, and wanting to write something to do with 'Shine On' *ie* something to do with a person succumbing to the pressures of life in general and rock 'n roll in particular . . . we'd just come off an American Tour when I wrote that, and I'd been exposed to all the boogaloo. . .

No, Roger . . . you must have written it after the English tour, because 'Have a Cigar' was included in 'Shine On' during the American Tour in April '75. . .
Oh yes! Right . . . I can't do it can I? This interview. My minds just a scrambled egg, mate. I can't answer these questions. I don't know! . . . I don't know the answers to the questions. I'll have to go home and study some more. I'm going to have to think about it all very carefully then I shall make a statement to the press about all this and that. God Peter, (Peter Barnes. Floyd Music Publisher, producing the Song Book) I'm sorry. I wanted to do this interview. I wanted it to be good, coherent, friendly interview for the punters but my mind's scrambled . . . no, my mind's not scrambled, I just can't get my mind round all that fucking nonsense . . . all that bollocks about when, how and why . . . you know, the medium is not the message, Marshall . . . is it? I mean, it's all in the lap of the fucking gods. . . (Pause for laughter)

Listen, Roger. What do you say to accusations about the album that you are biting the hand that feeds you . . . that the position you take up in a lot of the lyrics is highly dubious given the nature of your success?
Why? Biting the hand of the record companies?

Of the business . . .
Well the business doesn't feed me, you see. It's the people who buy the records who are doing the feeding. I mean, I like to believe that the people who buy the records listen to the lyrics and some of them some of the time think:- Yeah, that's fucking true, or there's a bit of truth in them somewhere, and that's all

that really matters. Some of the lyrics may even be directed at some of the record buyers. I don't think they are on this album, but they are in some of the songs I've written that aren't recorded yet. On the album they are mainly directed at a kind of inanimate being – the business. And the business doesn't feed us. The public feeds us; in spite of the business really. The public feed the business as well. The people who buy records feed everybody.

So the disillusionment implicit in the album, is only disillusionment with the business?

I never harboured any illusions so far as the business was concerned. I was under some illusions so far as the band was concerned. Like I was saying earlier about the guy in Genesis who thinks that there's something special about them . . . I think he said their music demands you listen to it, you can't carry on a conversation while its on. I know I felt like that about our music at one time 'cos I've listened to interviews I did, and sat and laughed myself sick listening to those. You know, twenty year old punks spouting a whole bunch of shit, a whole bunch of middle class shit, about "quality", making qualitative judgements about what we were doing. And when one or two pundits said that we were *real* music and a cut above your average rock 'n roll band, or set us apart from the mainstream of rock 'n roll as something rather special and important. I was very happy to believe it at the time. Of course it's absolute crap. Electric pop *is* where its at in terms of music today. Nobody's writing modern works for symphony orchestras that anybody's . . . well some people may be interested, but fucking few, and the divisions that always existed between popular music and serious music are no longer there. You can't get any more serious than Lennon at his most serious. If you get any more seious than *that* you fucking throw yourself under a train!

I'd like to know more about the early difficulties you had in the studio during 'Wish you were Here'.

I think having made it – having become very successful – was the starting point. But having made it, if we could all have accepted that's what we were in it for, we could then have all split up gracefully at that point. But we can't, and the reason we can't is, well there are several reasons. I haven't really thought about this very carefully, but I would say one reason is:- if you have a need to make it, to become, a super-hero in your own terms and a lot of other peoples as well, when you make it the need isn't dissipated – you still have the need, therefore you try to maintain your position as a superhero. I think that's true of all of us. Also, when you've been in a band eight years and you've all been working and plugging away to get to the top together its very frightening to leave, to do something else. Its nice and safe and warm and easy . . . basically its easy. If the four of us now got together and put out a record that didn't have our name attached to it it would be bloody difficult. The name 'Pink Floyd', the name not us, not the individuals in the band, but the name Pink Floyd is worth millions of pounds. The name is probably worth one million sales of an album, any album we put out. Even if we just coughed a million people will have ordered it simply

because of the name. And if anybody leaves, or we split up, its back to our own resources without the name. None of us are really sure of our resources; an awful lot of people in rock 'n roll aren't sure of their resources. That's why they're in there trying to prove they're big and loveable . . . I mean, I know I'm big and loveable, Nick, but I'm worried about some of the other chaps . . .

(Laughter) . . . that's why I stay in the group . . . I'm worried about the others, whats going to become of them . . . (More Laughter)

Having decided on bridging 'Shine On', the album then came quite easily, didn't it?

Yes. Quite quick and easy. 'Have a Cigar' first . . . actually some of the lyrics to 'Wish you were Here' came first. Just lyrics on a piece of paper, several couplets and pairs of words. That was kind of shelved, then 'Have a Cigar'. When we changed the plan we had a big meeting — we all sat round and unburdened ourselves a lot, and I took notes on what everybody was saying. It was a meeting about what wasn't happening and why. Dave was always clear that he wanted to do the other two songs — he never quite copped what I was talking about. But Rick did and Nicky did and he was outvoted so we went on.

The sessions were in two blocks, weren't they?

Two blocks. The middle of January to the middle of March. An American Tour, then another month (May) in the studio, another American Tour, then we came back and finished it off. Took three weeks, I think.

How much of your albums arise spontaneously in studio work, and how much is laid down before you ever record?

You can't really generalise. For example, 'Have a Cigar'. The verses, (tune and words) were all written before I ever played it to the others. Except the stuff before and after the vocal, that happened in the studio. The same with 'Welcome to the Machine' — the verses were done, but the run up and out was done in the studio. 'Dark Side' was done much more with us all working together. We all sat in a room for ages and ages — we'd got a whole lot of pieces of music and I put an idea over the whole thing and wrote the words. Having laid lyrics on the different bits we decided what order to put them in, and how to link them. It wasn't like the concept came first and then we worked right through it.

No rule then, about which comes first — the music or lyric?

No, except that either the music comes first and the lyrics are added, or music and lyrics come together. Only once have the lyrics been written down first — 'Wish you were Here'. But this is unusual; it hasn't happened before.

Why did you get Roy Harper to do the vocal on 'Have a Cigar'?

. . . a lot of people think I can't sing, including me a bit. I'm very unclear about what singing is. I know I find it hard to pitch, and I know the sound of my voice isn't very good in purely aesthetic terms, and Roy Harper was recording his own album in another EMI studio at the time, he's a mate, and we thought he could probably do a job on it.

Didn't you also use Stephane Grappelly on the album somewhere?

Yeah. He was downstairs when we were doing 'Wish you were Here'. Dave had

made the suggestion that there ought to be a country fiddle at the end of it, or we might try it out, and Stephane Grappelli was downstairs in number one studio making an album with Yehudi Menuhin. There was an Australian guy looking after Grappelli who we'd met on a tour so we thought we'd get Grappelli to do it. So they wheeled him up after much bartering about his fee — him being an old pro he tried to turn us over, and he did to a certain extent. But it was wonderful to have him come in and play a bit.

He's not on the album now, though?

You can just hear him if you listen very, very, very hard right at the end of 'Wish you were Here', you can just hear a violin come in after all the wind stuff starts — just! We decided not to give him a credit, 'cos we thought it might be a bit of an insult. He got his £300, though.

I want to ask about your own writing. Do you work at it? Do you sit down and think:- Ah! today I'll write a song?

Sometimes I do. Sometimes I think, RIGHT!, and go and pick up a guitar and occasionally it works. Usually something just flashes into my mind and I think, well, I better write this down and then I go and pick up the guitar. Usually a word, a phrase, a thought, or an idea. Once you've got five words or a series of words that contain an idea . . . like 'come in here, dear boy' then from that point on it becomes quite easy — or at least to do one verse. What's difficult is writing another verse, then another. The first is easy.

What about the two songs that weren't on the album.

I think we'll record those, and there's a couple of other songs I'd like the Floyd to record.

What? Another album in the next twelve months?

Oh yes, in the next few months. I've got a feeling we may knock another one off a bit sharpish . . . bang it out . . . O.K. you started asking me why two years after 'Dark Side', and "why not?" is how I feel about it. All this bloody nonsense in the press about "waiting for so long". Sure some people may have been waiting but it's only important 'cos a lot of people buy them. It's only important to the fucking papers and the pundits because a lot of people buy it.

Do you think the Floyd will do concerts again?

I've really no idea . . . not unless something fairly stupendous happens.

Do you personally want to do more with the Floyd?

I've been through a period when I've not wished to do any concerts with the Floyd ever again. I felt that very strongly, but the last week I've had vague kind of flickerings, feeling that I could maybe have a play. But when those flickerings hit the front of my mind I cast myself back into how fucking dreadful I felt on the last American Tour with all those thousands and thousands and thousands of drunken kids smashing each other to pieces. I felt dreadful because it had nothing to do with us — I didn't think there was any contact between us and them. There was no more contact between us and them than them and . . . I was just about to say the Rolling Stones and them. There obviously is contact of a kind between Mick Jagger and the public but its wierd and its not the kind of

contact that I want to be involved with really. I don't like it. I don't like all that Superstar hysteria. I don't like the idea of selling that kind of dream 'cos I know its unreal 'cos I'm there. I'm at the top . . . I am the dream and it ain't worth dreaming about. Not in the way they think it is anyway. It's all that "I want to be a rock 'n roll singer" number which rock 'n roll sells on. It sells partly on the music but it sells a hell of a lot on the fact that it pushes that dream.

A lot of people have made remarks to me over the album's sadness.

I'm glad about that . . . I think the world is a very, very sad fucking place . . . I find myself at the moment, backing away from it all . . . I'm very sad about Syd, I wasn't for years. For years I suppose he was a threat because of all that bollocks written about him and us. Of course he was very important and the band would never have fucking started without him because he was writing all the material. It couldn't have happened without him but on the other hand it couldn't have gone on *with* him. He may or may not be important in Rock 'n Roll anthology terms but he's certainly not nearly as important as people say in terms of Pink Floyd. So I think I was threatened by him. But when he came to the 'Wish you were Here' sessions — ironic in itself — to see this great, fat, bald, mad person, the first day he came I was in fucking tears . . . 'Shine On's' not really about Syd — he's just a symbol for all the extremes of absence some people have to indulge in because it's the only way they can cope with how fucking sad it is — modern life, to withdraw completely. And I found that terribly sad . . . I think finally that that maybe one of the reasons why we get slagged off so much now. I think it's got a lot to do with the fact that the people who write for the papers don't want to know about it because they're making a living from Rock 'n Roll.

And they don't want to know the real Barrett/Pink Floyd story.

Oh, they definitely don't want to know the real Barrett story . . . there are no facts involved in the Barrett story so you can make up any story you like — and they do. There's a vague basis in fact *ie* Syd was in the band and he did write the material on the first album, 80% of it, but that's all. It is only that one album, and that's what people don't realise. That first album, and one track on the second. That's all; nothing else.

Some of the reviews have been particularly scathing about 'Shine On' . . . calling it an insult to Syd.

Have they? I didn't see that, but I can imagine because its so easy for them. Its one of the very best king of rock 'n roll stories:- we are very successful and because we're very successful we're very vulnerable to attack and Syd is the weapon that is used to attack us. It makes it all a bit spicy — and that's what sells the papers that the people write for. But its also very easy because none of its fact — it's all hearsay and none of them *know* anything, and they all just make it up. Somebody makes it up once and the others believe it. All that stuff about Syd starting the space-rock thing is just so much fucking nonsense. He was completely into Hilaire Belloc, and all his stuff was kind of whimsical — all fairly heavy rooted in English literature. I think Syd had one song that had anything

to do with space — Astronomy Domine — that's all. That's the sum total of all Syd's writing about space and yet there's this whole fucking mystique about how he was the father of it all. It's just a load of old bollocks — it all happened afterwards. There's an instrumental track which we came up with together on the first album — 'Interstellar Overdrive' — thats just the title, you see, it's actually an abstract piece with an interstellar attachment in terms of its name. They don't give a shit anyway.

. . . I'm very pleased that people are copping the album's sadness, that gives me a doleful feeling of pleasure — that some of the people out there who are listening to it are getting it. Not like the cunts who are writing in the papers:- "gosh, well, we waited so long for this", and then start talking about the fucking guitar solo in wierd terms, and who obviously haven't understood what it's about. That guitar phrase of Dave's, the one that inspired the whole piece, *is* a very sad phrase. I think these are very mournful days. Things aren't getting better, they're getting worse and the seventies is a very baleful decade. God knows what the eighties will be like. The album *was* very difficult; it was a bloody difficult thing to do, and it didn't quite come off, but it nearly happened . . . difficult because of the first six weeks of the sessions *ie.* 'Shine On', not the sax solo which was put on afterwards, but the basic track was terribly fucking hard to do because we were all out of it and you can hear it. I could always hear it, kind of mechanical and heavy. That's why I'm so glad people are copping the sadness of it — that in spite of ourselves we did manage to get something down, we did manage to get something of what was going on in those sessions down on the vinyl. Once we accepted that we were going to go off on a tangent during the sessions it did become exciting, for me anyway, because then it was a desperate fucking battle trying to make it good. Actually we expended too much energy before that point in order to be able to quite do it. By the time we were finishing it, after the second American Tour, I hadn't got an ounce of creative energy left in me anywhere, and those last couple of weeks were a real fucking struggle.

The nightmare was simply all of you arriving at doing it, and not really knowing why?

Yes, absolutely. Which is why it's good. It's symbolic of what was going on. Most people's experience is arriving at a point at which others are arriving from somewhere else and not knowing what they're doing or why. And all we were doing making 'Wish you were Here' was being like everybody else — full of doubts and uncertainties. You know, we don't know whats happening either. . .

You were just fulfilling a contract?

Not really, because we don't have to make albums. Fulfilling a contract with ourselves if you like, because although legally we don't have to do anything, we do have to do something otherwise we'd all shoot ourselves.

Wish You Were Here

WATERS, GILMOUR

rail___
What have we found ___ the same___ old___ fears___   a smile___ from a   veil,___

Do you think you can tell ___   And did they get you to trade
Wish you___ were   here___

___ rail ___   your he - roes   for   ghosts,

hot ash - es   for   trees,___   hot air___ for a   cool_

26

breeze,   cold   com-fort for   charge

And did you   ex-change   a walk on   part in   the   war

   for a   lead   role   in   a   cage

Repeat and fade

Da da da da   da da da da da

Shine On You Crazy Diamond (Part I)

WRIGHT, WATERS, GILMOUR

Shine On You Crazy Diamond (Part II)

GILMOUR, WATERS, WRIGHT

Shine On You Crazy Diamond (Part III)

WATERS, GILMOUR, WRIGHT

34

Shine On You Crazy Diamond (Part IV)

GILMOUR, WRIGHT, WATERS

Shine On You Crazy Diamond (Part V)

WATERS

Re-member when you were young
reach-ed for the se-cret too soon
you
you

shone like the sun
cried for the moon
Shine on you

cra - zy dia - mond

Now there's a look in your eyes
Threatened by shad-ows at night
Like black
And ex -

far - a - way laugh - ter,   Come on,   you   strang - er, you   le - gend, you
se - er of   vi - sions,   Come on,   you   paint - er, you   pip - er, you

mart - yr and   shine!   *Instrumental*
prison-er and

you   shine!

Segue

Shine On You Crazy Diamond (Part VI)

WRIGHT, WATERS, GILMOUR

Shine On You Crazy Diamond (Part VII)

WATERS, GILMOUR, WRIGHT

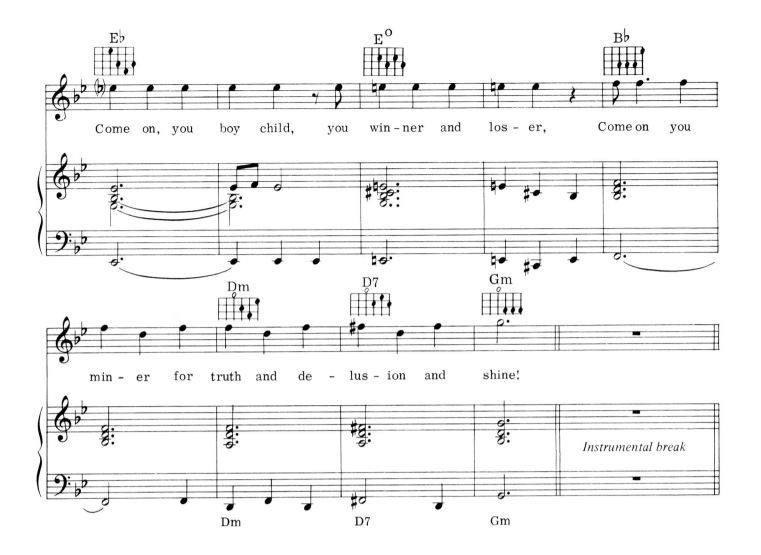

Come on, you boy child, you win-ner and los-er, Come on you min-er for truth and de-lus-ion and shine!

Instrumental break

Shine On You Crazy Diamond (Part VIII)

GILMOUR/WRIGHT/WATERS

*Repeat to fade
(ad lib. on theme)*

Shine On You Crazy Diamond (Part IX)

WRIGHT

Have A Cigar

WATERS

Come in here dear boy have a ci - gar you're gon-na go far,
We're just knocked out, We heard a-bout the sell out,

You're gon-na fly high, You're nev-er gon-na die, you're gon-na
You've got-ta get an al - bum out, you owe it to the peo-ple, we're so

make it if you try, they're gon-na love you,
hap - py we can hard - ly count,

Well I've al - ways had a deep respect and I mean that most sin - cere -
Ev'ry bo-dy else is just green

- ly
Have you seen the chart?
The band is just fan - tas -tic that is
It's a hell - u - va start__ it could be

real - ly what I think oh by the way, which one's pink?)
made in - to a mon-ster if we all pull to-geth- er as a team.)

And did we tell you the name of the game

boy,   We call it "Rid-ing the the ___ gravy

train" _____

Gtr. solo repeat ad lib.

55

Welcome To The Machine

WATERS

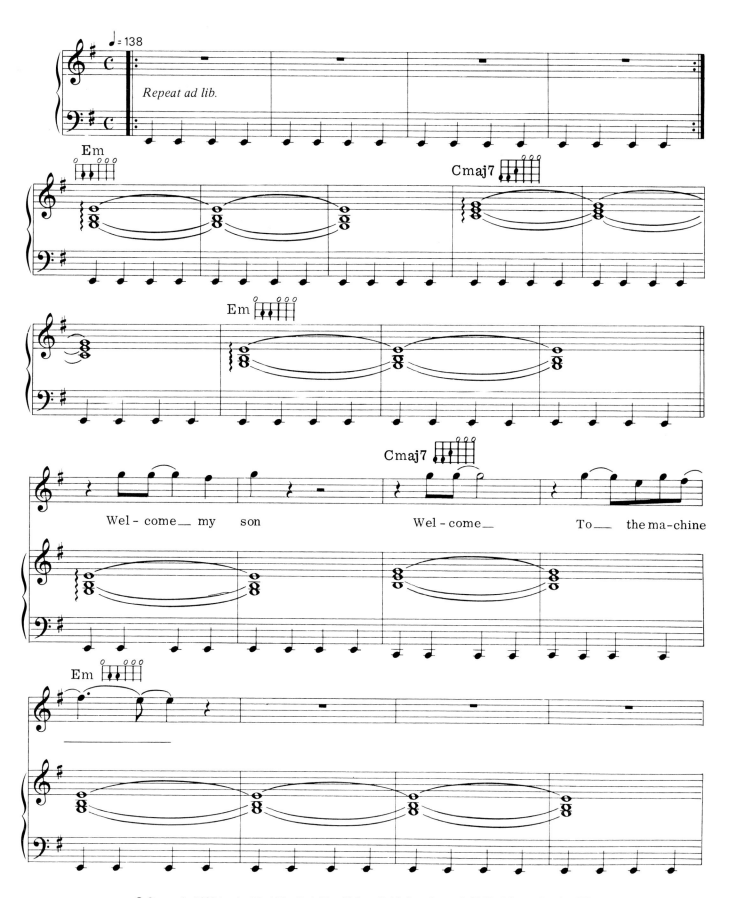

Wel - come__ my son   Wel - come__   To__ the ma-chine

You bought____ a guitar____ to pun-ish your ma____

And you did-n't like school ____ And you know you're no - bo-dy's fool ____

So wel - come ____

to____ the ma - chine ____

59

Wel - come __ my son wel - come __

to __ the ma - chine _____

al-ways ate __ in the steak __ bar,   He loved to drive __ in his Jag-

- uar,   So wel - come _____

_____ to __ the ma-chine _____

ad lib. synth.

Repeat and fade ad lib.

An Interview with David Gilmour by Gary Cooper

For any of today's bands — and Floyd are no exception — time spent in the recording studio is perhaps the most crucial aspect of their success. As studio techniques continue to develop, providing access to a variety of sounds and musical expression which were impossible before recent technological progress, many groups have come to rely increasingly on the facilities a studio has to offer.

A changing musical scene breeds a change of interest on the part of the public. As Pink Floyd have been consistently at the forefront of the shifting emphasis from hastily written, produced and recorded singles to extensively thought-out and intensively recorded albums, it has become essential to consider the way in which they are currently working.

Whereas an album was once cut from start to finish in a couple of days, 'Wish You Were Here' took from mid January 1975 through to July of the same year. In fairness, however, it should be pointed out that this lengthy session was broken for two American tours and rehearsals. During that period, the band worked more or less solidly from 2.30 every afternoon to well into the evening, stopping when they felt they'd had enough. This strict regime was kept up for four days a week.

The album was cut at EMI's massive Abbey Road Studios, which nestle quietly in a residential part of London's St. John's Wood. These studios are now a legend of course, having been the birthplace of many of rock's greatest albums, including much of the Beatles' and the Hollies' work. In spite of this, with so many other excellent studios around these days, the question remains as to why Floyd prefer Abbey Road. For the answer to this question and many others, we spoke to David Gilmour.

"We've always used it. We've done virtually every album there. I think it's pretty much a thing of habit but we do tend to use a lot of electronic facilities and some of the smaller studios just haven't got the equipment to cope with the various things we want to do. Unless you've got a good reason to go somewhere else, you don't go anywhere else, do you?"

The whole idea of 'Wish You Were Here' came out of rehearsals in a room in King's Cross. Those ideas became the basis of "Shine On You Crazy Diamond," which was performed on tour in France and England. It's intriguing to hear how Shine On was actually recorded and how the rest of the numbers were composed and added to complete the album.

"First of all we did a basic track of "Shine On You Crazy Diamond" from the beginning where the first guitar solo starts, right through Shine On and the part with the sax solo through to the continuation of Shine On. That was in all twenty minutes long, which was at one time going to be the whole of one side of the album. However, as we worked on it and extended it and then extracted things, we came to the decision that we would make that into the whole album and we began to work on the new stuff to slot in."

Here, Floyd are basically following the standard practise of laying down a backing track comprising bass, drums and guitar, possibly with keyboards added. They take the idea one step further, however, by extending the practise from a single track to the whole album. Then they separate the backing track and insert later ideas, carefully polishing and refining until they are ready to mix down the ammassed ideas onto two tracks for the two channels of a stereo system.

All this sounds very smooth running and straightforward, but the recording of that particular backing track was not without its attendant problems. They were forced to spend a whole week trying to get the exact drum sound that they wanted and a few other things held up the proceedings, too, as David explains.

"We originally did the backing track over the course of several days, but we came to the conclusion that it just wasn't good enough. So we did it again in one day flat and got it a lot better. Unfortunately nobody understood the desk properly and when we played it back we found that someone had switched the echo returns from monitors to tracks one and two. That affected the tom-toms and guitars and keyboards which were playing along at the time. There was no way of saving it, so we just had to do it yet again."

Like most bands today, Floyd rarely recorded anything 'live'. In other words, they tend not to be all playing at once. A rhythm track is laid down and the embellishments added later. But there are some tracks which are more or less live in the studio. "Have A Cigar" was a whole track on which I used the guitar and keyboards at once. There are some extra guitars which I dubbed on later, but I did the basic guitar tracks at one time," explained David.

Floyd chose that technique as being the one that best fitted the nature of the song itself. This total awareness of differing material and techniques also extends itself to "Welcome To The Machine," a totally different type of number to "Have A Cigar," on which they employed a radically different approach.

"It's very much a made-up-in-the-studio thing which was all built up from a basic throbbing made on a VCS 3, with a one repeat echo used so that each 'boom' is followed by an echo repeat to give the throb. With a number like that, you don't start off with a regular concept of group structure or anything, and there's no backing track either. Really it is just a studio proposition where we're using tape for its own ends — a form of collage using sound."

The number "Welcome To The Machine" posed another problem one familiar to a lot of bands — recording synthesisers. With any electronic instrument, you have the choice of playing it through an amplifier taking your tonal colouration from the amplifier, or playing straight through the mixing desk, a technique known as direct injection. Floyd normally direct inject the bass and keyboards and Gilmour occasionally D.I.'s the guitar. Synthesisers, however, create their own problems, as David pointed out.

"It's very hard to get a full synthesiser tone down on tape. If you listen to them before and after they've been recorded, you'll notice that you've lost a lot. And although I like the sound of a synthesiser through an amp, you still lose something that way as well. Eventually what we decided to do was to use D.I. on synthesiser because that way you don't increase your losses and the final result sounds very much like a synthesiser through a stage amp."

In mythological terms Floyd are often thought of as being perhaps the major users of new effects and studio techniques. Yet this is something Gilmour denies strongly.

"I don't think we use new equipment all that much. We do use a lot of studio effects but none of them are particularly new. Most of them are recorded by using all the old regular equipment. There are millions of different effects you can produce just by using a tape recorder or two. You can do phasing, automatic double tracking, sound on sound, most things in fact."

Incredible as it may sound, there are quite a few electronic devices on the market that Floyd haven't begun to experiment with yet, such as digital delay units for phasing and ADT. They prefer to do things the slow way with two tape machines, rather than employ the newer electronic methods. Yet in spite of this unwillingness to dispense with tried and trusted techniques, their use of effects is impressive to say the least.

When a track disappears into a thin, reedy transistor radio sound which is then joined by a plainly recorded acoustic guitar, there has obviously been a lot of thought behind the end product. How did they tackle that one?

"When it sounds like it's coming out of a radio, it was done by equalisation. We just made a copy of the mix and ran it through eq. to make it very middly, knocking out all the bass and most of the high top so that it sounds radio-like. The interference was recorded on my car cassette radio and all we did was to put that track on top of the original track. It's all meant to sound like the first track getting sucked into a radio with one person sitting in the room playing guitar along with the radio."

Studio equipment can also be useful in helping you out of a tight spot, especially with vocals, which is where Floyd found they needed a bit of first-aid. Varying the tape speed is one cure.

"We have quite a bit of difficulty with vocals. I have trouble with the quality of my voice but I don't have much difficulty keeping in tune. On the other hand, Roger has no problem with vocal quality but he does have trouble keeping in tune."

Normally Floyd will keep working away at a vocal line until it's right. There was one track, though, which just refused to go the way they wanted it.

"The only time we've ever used tape speed to help us with vocals was on one line of The Machine Song. It was a line I just couldn't reach so we dropped the tape down half a semitone and then dropped the line in on the track."

All this takes a lot of time, but what takes Floyd even longer is the actual process of adding and subtracting ideas on their basic 24 tracks on the tape machine. Eventually these are all mixed down (an acoustic blending operation) to the basic two tracks, but not until everything you need has gone down on the 24. Dave expanded on this subject.

"We go on and on adding things and throwing things away and it all changes while you're doing that. In the end when you mix it's simply a process of choosing what you will emphasise at any one time. You've got all the tracks there but you'll bring just one thing forward at one time and subdue it later on."

Strangely enough, Gilmour claims that mixing these results of months of hard creative work is a quick operation.

"It took us about a week on this album. We do get into a lot of arguments about the way things should be mixed and sometimes it comes down to two people mixing it differently and then we vote to see which mix to use."

Usually the majority of the band is present on mixing sessions, but with one person actually taking the producer's chair. In Gilmour's case this is also the engineer's chair as he prefers to do the balancing of the tracks he's mixing himself.

It's only quite recently that 24 track started being widely used. Some major UK studios have only just expanded from 16 to 24 tracks and some have still to install their new 24 track machines. Yet, while 24 tracks is still a new toy to play with, Gilmour already foresees a move beyond it.

"We have never needed more than 24 tracks as yet. It could easily happen, though, because as one gets into quad everything multiplies. One track is just one track for mono, but you need two for stereo and four tracks for one track of quad, so you could easily find yourself short of tracks on 24 tracks with quad."

In some ways 'Wish You Were Here' is a rather bare album from the point of view of effects and studio gimmicks, the time spent on its recording having been taken up more with the overall painting of the sound — a creative effort over the long months finally made into a complete whole by selection. Obviously studio technique assists Pink Floyd in no small way, but it would not appear to be an end in itself.

PINK FLOYD
WISH YOU WERE HERE
Album No. Harvest SHVL 814
Recorded at Abbey Road Studios
January to July 1975
Album released September 1975

This book designed by Hipgnosis
Photographs by Jill Furmanovsky, Storm Thorgerson,
Peter Christopherson and Po
Graphics by George Hardie N.T.A. and Richard Evans
Guitar transcriptions by Colgan Bryan

Published by Pink Floyd Music Publishers Ltd.,
27 Noel Street, London W1V 3RD.

All tour photographs taken during the British Tour of November 1974

Other photographs taken during the album cover photographed in May and June 1975

Exclusive Distributors:
Music Sales Corporation
257 Park Avenue South, New York, NY 10010

Music Sales Limited
8/9 Frith Street, London W1V 5TZ England

Music Sales Pty. Limited
120 Rothschild Street, Rosebery, Sydney, NSW 2018, Australia

Order No. AM 64189
(US) ISBN 0.8256.1079.6
(UK) ISBN 0.7119.1029.4

Printed in the United States of America by Vicks Lithograph and Printing Corporation